Christmas 1989

Jim

IMPRESSIONS of BRISTOL

ACKNOWLEDGEMENTS

Michael B Edwards would like to thank everyone who so willingly helped with the project particularly Shani Hempstead for her research and drafting of the commentary, Roy Hill for his invaluable advice and guidance and Sybil Edwards for her enthusiasm and active involvement over four years of preparation.

First published 1989 by

Fragonard Publishing
40 Caledonia Place
Clifton Bristol

ISBN 0 9515052 0 3

Book design & jacket by John Buchmuller of Baseline Creative.
Printed by Bath Midway Litho Limited, England.

IMPRESSIONS of BRISTOL

Paintings and drawings
by Michael B Edwards

FRAGONARD PUBLISHING

IMPRESSIONS of BRISTOL

Much has been written about many aspects of the City of Bristol, its architecture, history, industry, people and culture and yet above all Bristol is a visually exciting city. It has the fascination of the harbour with its tall ships and modern yachts and its bustling water-front of shops and pubs. There is the elegance and sophistication of Clifton and the beauty of the Gorge and of the Suspension Bridge and finally the City itself with glimpses of a prosperous merchant past set against the modern skyline.

I have painted these pictures over a period of four years and already a few are a record of past history with the continual change which inevitably occurs in any dynamic city.

My interpretations are of course very personal, but I hope they contain some interesting perceptions, even for those who know the City well. For visitors or newcomers to Bristol or those interested in gaining some understanding of the City from afar, I hope this book will provide an overall impression of the appearance and diversity of Bristol.

The architectural features of Bristol are more to be found in the detail of individual buildings or locations rather than in the totality of the City.

The Watershed

While its neighbour Bath is consistently Georgian in style, and perhaps museum-like in atmosphere, Bristol's architectural highlights exist in pockets or individual buildings. For example, the Georgian terraces in Clifton rival Bath's, but are intermixed with Victorian and contemporary developments. The Victorian warehouses along Welsh Back by the Harbour offer, individually, a wealth of attention to detail and surface texturing while St Mary Redcliffe Church, described by Queen Elizabeth I as the most beautiful parish church in England, is now squashed between a less than memorable hotel building and a car park. There are more gems to be found, depending on individual preferences, and I include some of them in these pages.

This book concentrates on the visual aspects of Bristol with a selection, regrettably limited, of those parts of the City, many well known and some less so, that have caught my eye as an artist. There are many other parts of the City which are not included which doubtless will be missed but the objective is not to provide a comprehensive guide, which many other publications do well, but to highlight a few of the visual gems of Bristol.

Bristol is a city of contrasts: of arts and science, of hill tops and gorge, skyscrapers and ancient monuments. For the artist, in all of this, there is a fascination of contrasts, of light and shade, texture, colours and atmosphere, which add up to an ambience which is uniquely Bristol's. The reflections in the harbour, the sepia of the crowded market halls or the quiet cool shades of the cathedral all provide a subject for brush on canvas or pen on paper. The range is tremendous.

Three major areas of considerable contrast are featured in this book: the City, the Harbour and Clifton. Each has its own distinctive personality and contributes a major part to the overall character of Bristol.

The Cathedral

From across the Green, the Cathedral provides a massive and solid presence. Smaller than many other cathedrals, the building dates from the twelfth century, with a number of subsequent additions. Its eastern extremity contains the most important architectural features, the nave and towers to the west being Victorian but of medieval design to complete a unified and beautiful building.

The western face of the Cathedral catches the light from midday to evening, the changing light patterns providing tones, colours and textures, of fascination to painters and public alike and perhaps enriched by the nearby reflected light from the harbour. The west of the Cathedral is often missed by the passing motorist.

The West Face

From the noise of the traffic around College Green and the hustle and bustle of the City one can step into another world: the quietness, dignity and spiritual sanctity of the Cathedral's interior. Warm light from the south floods the altar and choir, while a cool northern light catches the columns along the aisles and lights up the edge of the rood screen.

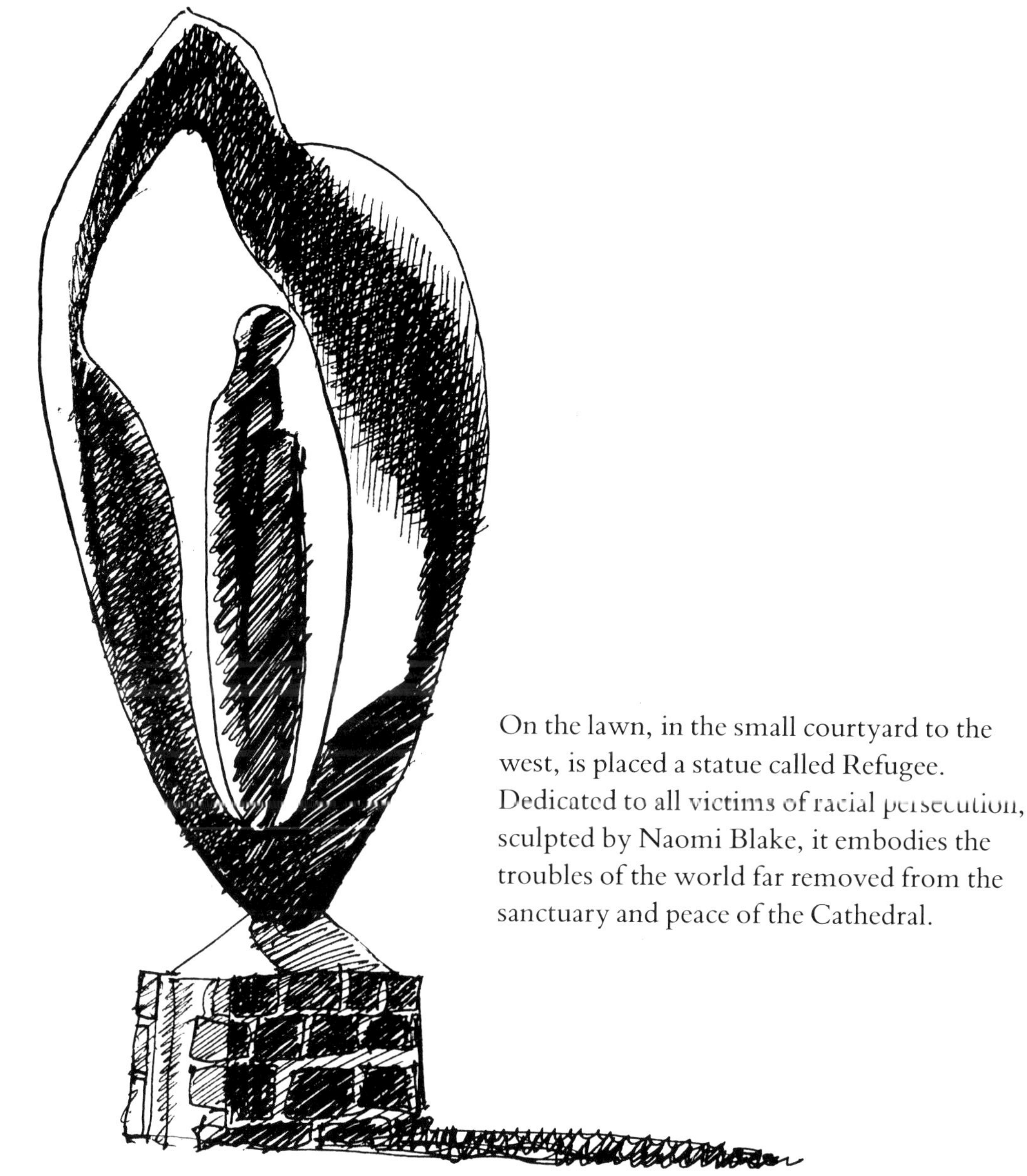

On the lawn, in the small courtyard to the west, is placed a statue called Refugee. Dedicated to all victims of racial persecution, sculpted by Naomi Blake, it embodies the troubles of the world far removed from the sanctuary and peace of the Cathedral.

St Nicholas Market

St Nicholas Market is a place to discover for oneself. There is no vantage point, but from within. In a sense it is like a grotto: from the outside unnoticed, but from within a place of both robust and gentle charm. Approached from the passages of Corn Street it comes as a surprise, perhaps more so today than in former times when it would have been a busier and noisier thoroughfare.

St Nicholas Market from Corn Street

Interior of St Nicholas Market

The essence of the market is its delicate structures, the iron girders pressing glass against the sky, a giant skylight designed to house the street traders who in Victorian times cluttered up the streets. The large balloon-style lights illustrate a kind sensitivity to the coordination and design of that age.

Very near to St Nicholas Church, as well as the harbour and Bristol Bridge, the market provides a direct echo of Bristol's merchant trading ancestry. Even today the traders continue to sell a wide range of wares, from horticultural products and antiques to parts for vacuum cleaners.

St Nicholas Church can be seen through the passages around the market. But it now functions as a museum instead of a place of worship, concentrating on drawings and paintings of early Bristol, together with items of ecclesiastical history.

Corn Street

This is the heart of Bristol's business centre and one of the most famous views of the City. Usually in shadow from the Exchange building on the right, here I caught the sun casting a corridor of light across the pedestrian precinct to illuminate the extravagant architecture of the Lloyds Bank building on the left. Built in Victorian days, it was inspired by a Venetian library. The building is highly decorated, both inside and out, with sculptures, reliefs and friezes.

Although Corn Street was heavily bombed in the War, the Exchange the best example of 18th and 19th Century opulence survived, together with the phrase it became associated with – "to pay on the nail". Bargains were struck on the engraved bronze pillars or trading tables which now stand along the Exchange frontage.

Broad Street

Built on the Old City Wall, St John's Church is now surrounded by office blocks and contemporary buildings. Nevertheless, its position across the end of Broad Street ensures that it is not lost in modern architectural mediocrity. The gateway underneath the spire is the only medieval gateway left in existence through which Elizabeth I is reputed to have ridden when visiting the City.

Christmas Steps

This steep pedestrian passage connects two busy throughfares by a series of mishapen, uneven steps and cobbled paths with small shops, restaurants and pubs on either side. With old lamp posts, shop signs and a multiplicity of windows, doorways and rooflines, Christmas steps provides a small but dramatic reminder of a medieval past.

The light casts deep shadows and dramatic highlights, lifting each cobblestone into view and creating colours and shapes from the paving stones, old brick walls and painted shop fronts.

At the bottom of Christmas Steps is a redeveloped area, which incorporates old and new into a space which has an intimate human scale. Benches and tables are occupied by exhausted shoppers, lively children and passers-by enjoying a drink or food from the delightfully named Three Sugar Loaves pub.

St Michael's Hill

Viewed on a soft summer's day, St Michael's Hill provides a view of the City beyond, framed by the bay windows of the houses stepped up the hill. The wide elevated pavement, a mixture of paving stones and local red cobblestones, provides a safe path for pedestrians to walk, clear of the often heavy traffic. (Painting in any town is often much easier on Sundays, when there is little traffic and few pedestrians.) St Michael's Hill is a favourite spot in Bristol, with its seventeenth and eighteenth century houses of contrasting styles. Opposite the bay windows on the east side of the street are the stylish buildings and courtyard of Colston's Almshouses, very different from the modest accommodation one normally associates with such places.

Houses at the bottom of St Michael's Hill are painted yellow, red and white with large bay windows. These reminders of the past with the projecting floors above the street are ubiquitous features of the City. Many rows of such houses with the top storeys close enough for neighbours to shake hands across the street disappeared during the blitz.

The remainder have been converted into attractive cafes, shops and restaurants. On St Michael's Hill a good example is Sur La Colline, a French style restaurant with an attractive interior.

Close by St Michael's church stands this attractive house, with pointed mullioned windows, the plaster of the walls, dark red in colour, and the house facing onto the continuation of the pavement from St Michael's Hill. It is typical of the gems of old houses tucked away from sight in several parts of the centre of the City.

The Spectrum Building

Modern Bristol

In total contrast to the previous depiction of historical buildings, there is the technology of twentieth century construction. Such is the Spectrum Building dating from the 1980s. It provides a hi-tech entrance to Bristol from the M32. The blue tinted rectangles of glass reflect the city scape beyond. At night the entrance hall is illuminated by neon lights, tracing its clean cut modern arches like a glow-worm. While this piece of Manhattan in miniature seems out of context in provincial Bristol, it helps to off-set the debased architecture of the Broadmead Shopping Centre opposite.

More recently modern architecture in Bristol has tried to break away from the predictable tower block approach of the sixties and seventies. The Redcliffe Street buildings at the harbour's edge, facing Welsh Back, are suitably reminiscent of the buildings of the area. These were the red brick warehouses, stalwarts of commercial life, and fortunately some of these are still standing a few hundred yards further along. It's as though this older Victorian set has welcomed the new. Together they present a united front and a successful disguise, for they contain acres of offices which belie the 'warehouse' architectural theme!

King Street

The wide cobbled thoroughfare close to the docks, is the home of the Theatre Royal and Old Vic. As with London's Globe and the Rose, the theatre tradition grew up close to the people. But it seems an odd juxtaposition, the theatre flanked by the zig-zag roofs of rows of almshouses. A little too proud perhaps its pediment, standing much taller, much grander, than its humble neighbours. In fact, this pediment has been adopted by the Theatre. Originally it belonged to Coopers' Hall.

On the day when this was painted, the players of my canvas had the spotlight of the afternoon sun. The composition seemed to demand centre stage for the Theatre Royal. The contrast with the shape of the roofs was a dramatic and stark subject.

King Street is also a mecca for traditional jazz enthusiasts, drawn to the Old Duke pub, where the beat of Dixieland music poop-poop-a-doops across the cobbles.

Across the harbour, at the bottom of Kings Street, the original Welsh Back warehouses seem ignorant of their state of dereliction. The empty windows do not stare with the hollow vacant expression of a worthless cast-a-way. It seemed that I should try and record this healthy attitude! My example here is a burnt out warehouse and since its painting it has been developed into a fashionable apartment block. A just reward for such an architectural personality.

The brickwork and decoration of the warehouses demonstrate a previous generation's pride in their commercial buildings, so different from todays 'sheds'. Its tall, almost statuesque, nature adds much character to the Welsh Back environment and the preservation of a whole row of warehouses is one of the better aspects of modern Bristol's development.

Standing opposite the Old Duke is Bristol's most famous old building, the Llandoger Trow, which was named after the local flat-bottomed boats. Some of its fame is no doubt derived from its reputed connections with both Robert Louis Stevenson and Daniel Defoe. Now a pub and restaurant, it provides Bristol's principal example of timber framing. To the artist, such buildings are always tempting material. The strong black lines of jutting bay frontages, recesses and gabled roofs seem naturally suited to pen and ink. Drawing is always good practice and as I get going, I get carried away – somehow overtaken by Dickensian imagery, which seems to demand more detail than the simple sketch I had originally intended!

The Llandoger Trow

Brunel is one of the world's most famous engineers. His legacy in Bristol includes the most notable features of this City: Clifton Suspension Bridge, S.S. Great Britain, his original hotel and Temple Meads railway station. His designer's eye was as shrewd as his engineering know-how. His rather modest statue by John Doubleday is placed incongrously next to buildings which would have benefitted from his architecture and inspiration.

Queen Square

The Queen Square was built for prosperous and commercial business men by the City of Bristol and named in honour of Queen Anne's visit to the City in 1702. What I have tried to capture is the size and visual harmony of the square, which could not be done while the trees were in leaf !

The visual atmosphere is tranquil. Colour of building materials, storey heights, even lines and proportions to guide the eye were all strictly regulated, so that the intentions of the architect could be carried out to the letter.

The Georgians got things so right! How unfortunate that the tranquillity of Bristol's most elegant square has been disrupted by a major road which speeds past the fine equestrian statue of William III by Rysbrack.

I decided my representation would ignore the traffic, so here you see the north façade. In the cooler months of winter the character is more evident.

These gentle, warm, soft hues bring about a transformation as the leafy foreground slowly disrobes.

The square was damaged by the original Bristol riots and much later by the war. Fortunately, rebuilding has been in sympathy. The original objective has mostly been honoured.

Balloon Festival

Bristol is now a centre of ballooning at the Ashton Court Estate and the complex processes of inflation and launching are watched by many spectators.

The lyricism of their colours and shapes make compulsive viewing as they drift with the prevailing air streams on summer mornings and evenings.

At closer range, they have a more 'pop' art flavour. I enjoyed this quick sketch at a launching at Ashton Court. At Balloon Festival time, this natural amphitheatre sports hundreds of balloons at different stages of growth and development, like psychedelic mushrooms popping out of the ground!

Stapleton River

One of the surprises of suburban Bristol is the Stapleton River, a tree lined valley winding through the modern housing estates of Frenchay and Stapleton much today as it must have been in Danby's time. I had seen Danby's paintings recently at the City Museum, so I was keen to discover 'his Bristol'. Possibly the pool he painted where children played with toy boats might still be recognised. Retracing his steps and smelling the musty scent of the cool shady woods was like seeing his canvas before me. Danby painted Stapleton River on many occasions. Other subjects included ladies promenading or just landscapes of tree-lined waters with clear and vibrant light reflected from the river.

It made a change from the Avon Gorge, which was a heavily over subscribed subject for most painters in Bristol. Indeed this was the extraordinary landscape that had attracted so many artists throughout the 18th century. However, the Gorge could not lure all of the eminent portrait painters of the age; certainly not Gainsborough. The fashionable society over in Bath more than guaranteed his interest and attention.

Works of sculpture are evident throughout the City. Most are clear representations of historical figures, but the horse rider at the front of Christmas Steps is something different. It is not about someone we might recognise. It seems to be about a 'state of mind'. It communicates its message so powerfully that I always feel very drawn to it. This is the 'Cloaked horseman' by David Backhouse.

The artistic tradition is strong in Bristol and it serves a thriving artistic community. Not only the RWA, but also galleries such as the Eye Gallery, 3D, Pelter Sands, Alexander, Arnolfini and a number of others ensure that the tradition continues.

Junction Lock

THE HARBOUR

The skyline of Bristol, I think, is best seen from the harbourside, with the juxtaposition of the Cathedral, Wills Tower, skyscrapers, warehouses, offices and hotels a harmonious profile reflected in the harbour water. The boats moored alongside the harbour walls are an exciting addition. The view, overleaf, was only available between the time of demolishing the bonded warehouses at Canons Marsh and the building of the new Lloyds Bank offices.

The harbour is referred to as the 'Floating Harbour', but not because it actually floats! In earlier days, the tidal nature of the Avon left ships on the mud at low tide. Hence, when the lock gates were introduced and the ships floated for a full twenty four hours, it was transformed into a floating harbour.

Its presence in the centre of Bristol creates an immense point of interest and fascination.

It is the City's mirror. Light, movement and reflections – it plays back what it sees, but in a different way, like an orchestra modulating into a different key to re-state a theme. Not only artists, but people generally, are drawn to it for its contrast of scene, the boats and the variety of activities it offers. No one lives in Bristol oblivious to the harbour.

The harbour at Welsh Back is close to the heart of the city where once ships unloaded onto the dockside.

While Bristol is no longer a commercial port, apart from the ships of a sand-carrying company and the Wessex Water ship which are regular visitors, it still attracts a varied collection of boats: tall ships, yachts and modern racing speed boats.

The habour by Bristol Bridge

The Mayflower was the first steam tug, built in 1898, and it's still in commission for sightseeing trips around the harbour. As part of the industrial museum's collection, it lies moored alongside other historic craft, with the cranes of the past dock days towering overhead.

This picture was painted on a still grey autumn day. It was an unusual atmosphere – soft, calm, with not many people about. The mood is reflected in soft grey tones, pinks and yellow ochres. The watery reflections of the boats on the grey harbour match the greyness of the skyline with the occasional onlooker taking a late season walk along the dockside.

John Cabot

I had to include this statue of Cabot by Stephen Joyce erected in 1985. The fact that he crouches, larger than life, in this rustic style, clearly conveys what must have been his lust for adventure. Sited on the harbour front, just outside the Arnolfini, he is looking seaward. The bronze blends naturally with the cobble stones and in the distance stands the industrial museum and historic cranes.

The Lightship

On a still winter morning, the early light silhouettes the Lightship against a pale cerulean sky. Long shadows from the bench, and its occupant, stretch onto the cobbles. The tramp stirs – grudgingly – the fight to keep warm while sleeping out makes slumber uneasy. In a few hours time the Lightship will open its doors to serve food and drink. After a life of drama on the high seas, this is easy retirement.

GLASS BOAT

Another floating conversion is the Glass Boat Restaurant. This is moored a short distance from the Lightship and near the Bristol Bridge. It is now one of Bristol's more distinguished eating establishments. The style of the conversion supports its rather 'up market' ambience. I visualise it steaming up one of the lakes in the Lake District – grandly dressed sightseers aboard with binoculars raised to scan the bird life and lake shore.

Rather dramatic publicity surrounded the conversion of another working ship now called the Thekla. This was a coaster from the North that was sailed to Bristol and converted into a floating theatre bar. A number of teething problems and disputes were reported before the Thekla finally became an established part of the Bristol night-time scene.

St Mary Redcliffe

The vista of St Mary Redcliffe is a classic. The church itself is outstanding, and from this particular vantage point, on the harbour, its elegant spire is the focus of attention.

As I painted on this particular winter's morning, there was a sharpness in the air, producing almost photographic clarity.

The boat in the right foreground is the Glevum Art Gallery specialising in contemporary marine pictures by local artists.

St Mary Redcliffe is Bristol's architectural masterpiece. Even before stepping inside, the highly decorated porch can steal your attention. It seems to be almost oriental in its complexity. The interior has a character not found in other churches. Somehow the pillars have a soaring grace; it seems more spacious, loftier. The spire, its crown and glory, was added in 1872 after the original had been destroyed by lightning in 1446. Some of the stones on the north side, facing the busy inner ring road, have developed a green covering of lichen, which combines very pleasingly with some that are a discoloured dark grey tone and others that are yellow ochre and a lighter grey. I like the way nature has added its own decoration to this inspired building.

Bathhurst Basin is the ultimate cameo, my favourite waterside spot. It is at once picturesque, intimate and inspiring. Lining the basin is a colourful parade of Georgian houses with some tasteful modern infills. These face out to the water and to the boats. All of this on the doorstep of the Metropolis. A feast for a yachtman's eye as well as a painter's.

The church stands in the wings to some degree, likening the harbour to a village green setting. Just off the left hand side of the painting is a hospital. So the basin is a well serviced community particularly when you add the Ostrich pub.

S.S. Great Britain

From this bleak winter scene the familiar sight of the S.S. Great Britain greets the morning from her dry dock. The sun is beginning to strain through the grey mist and cloud as the City wakes up.

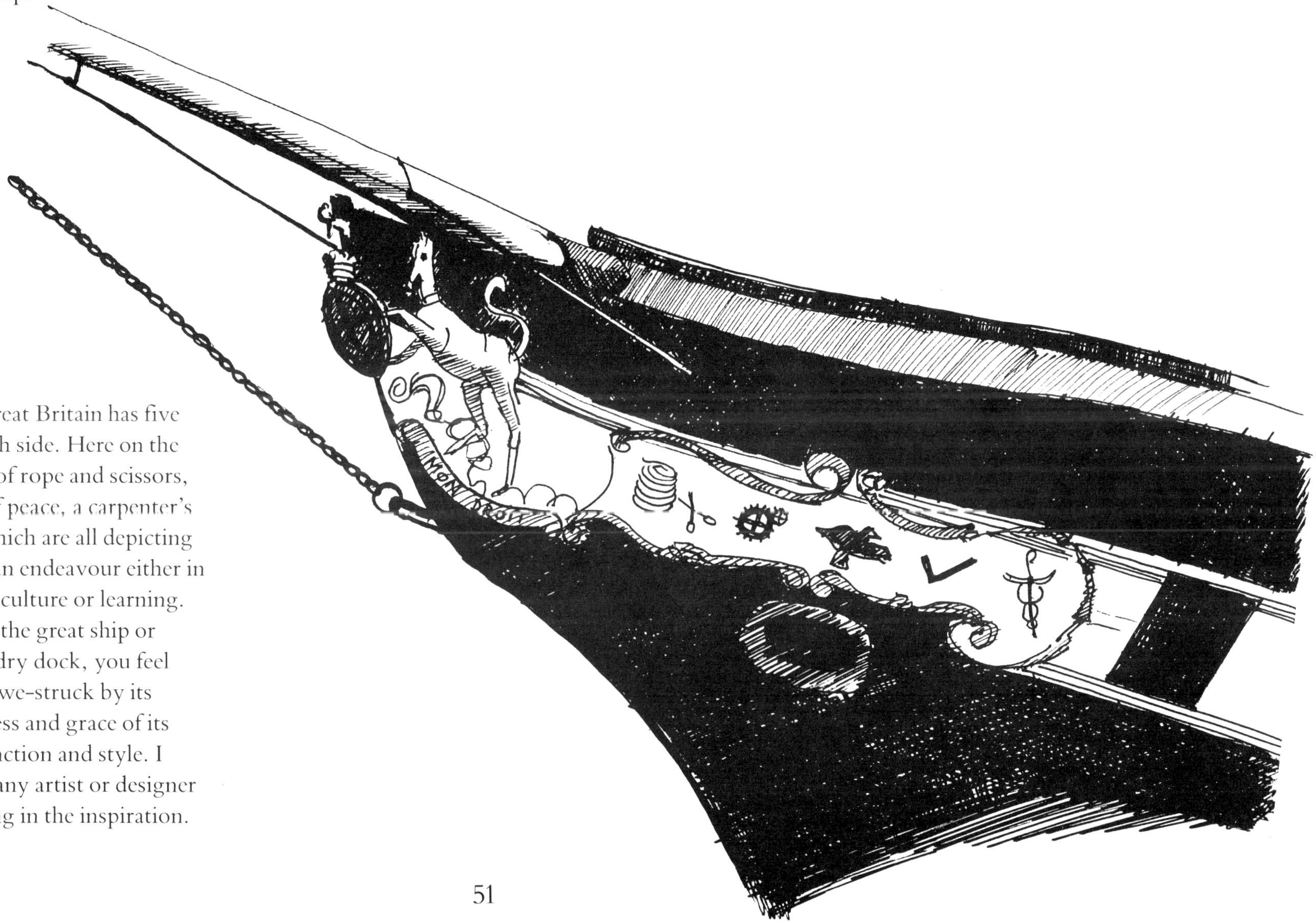

The prow of the S.S. Great Britain has five symbols carved into each side. Here on the port side they are a coil of rope and scissors, gear wheels, the dove of peace, a carpenter's square and Caduceus which are all depicting some aspects of Victorian endeavour either in the arts or industry, agriculture or learning.

Walking through the great ship or around its perimeter in dry dock, you feel both miniaturised and awe-struck by its enormity. The shapeliness and grace of its bulk is a marriage of function and style. I don't think I am alone, any artist or designer could spend days soaking in the inspiration.

House in West Mall

CLIFTON

The loveliest suburb in all of England was how John Betjeman once described Clifton and he would surely say the same today, for apart from the ever increasing overload of traffic and parked cars, Clifton continues to be cossetted, restored and renovated. Behind every stand of scaffolding, every sheet of builder's canvas or polythene, there is the promise of a re-emergence of some gem of Clifton's heritage.

Clifton Village is a name much promoted by estate agents and describes the historic centre of Clifton. A village it was, prior to the eighteenth century, on the outskirts of Bristol and, like Bath, the Georgian terraces of Clifton were built during a relatively short timescale. This was halted in mid-stream by the economic depression of the late 18th Century, before its final completion.

The long terraces of sand coloured stone, following the hillsides often in crescent shapes, have a form and beauty never captured again by architects in modern times. Clinging to the front elevations are often cast iron balconies with much wrought iron decoration – swirls, circles, leaf motifs, diamonds – the blacksmith craftsmen of the 1830's had an enviable skill in their ability to create such delicate tracery. Clifton's Georgian theme is set off by open spaces, with lawns and greens providing a changing backdrop through the seasons. Fresh green springs, deep green summers and golden autumns. For me, particularly with my architectural interest, Clifton is a treasure trove of inspiration.

Unlike Bath, which has the continuity and integration of a vastly constructed set piece, Clifton is a series of cameos. Royal York Crescent, the longest crescent ever built, its quite different in character from the Paragon, which itself differs markedly from the Pentagon or Cornwallis Crescent. Similarly, Vyvyan Terrace and West Mall, although of Georgian design are each expressing their individual aspects of the theme.

The character of Clifton comes not only from the grand façades and terraces, but also from the pubs, shops, boutiques and antiques market, together with the small cottages and mews houses, which all cluster together in the centre.

Unlike the surrounding areas sporting the larger single dwellings of Victorian Clifton which seem more remote and less involved, the centre of Clifton is always active and lively. A resident of Clifton Village confronts it immediately upon stepping outside his front door. No garden separates the front door from the street. Residents, students and tourists alike mingle on the pavement, a cosmopolitan concoction. Similar perhaps to London's Chelsea or Hampstead, with a bit of country atmosphere thrown in.

The boundary of Clifton on the South, is the Gorge. In fact the development of Clifton spread from the popularity of Hotwells, just below Clifton at the base of the Gorge. This fashionable watering place, somewhat akin to the Roman Baths in Bath, drew many visitors in the eighteenth century, and led to the development of the small village of Clifton, which later developed into this elegant Georgian and Regency community.

The Gorge which falls sheer from Clifton's boundary, 250 feet to the Avon below, provides a dramatic surprise for visitors. The sudden discovery of this precipice and view from Sion Hill or the Downs never fails to enchant.

For the artist, through the centuries, the Gorge has always been a challenge and with the addition of the bridge suspended high above the Avon River, there is an illusion of even greater height. This is the sight which has become Bristol's leading signature theme. To the west and north, Clifton's boundary is the Downs, a wide expanse of grass and trees which enhances Clifton's country character. This, as well as the Gorge's sharply defined boundary, serves to separate it from neighbours such as Sneyd Park or Stoke Bishop.

In this section of the book I've wanted to show Clifton throughout the seasons, to capture the changing light, the colours and the atmosphere year round.

Christchurch Green looking towards Canynge Road.

The Assembly Rooms

At the Victoria Assembly Rooms you have found Clifton's front porch! It is the first important architectural feature as you approach this part of Bristol. And what a portico it has too! It has outgrown the building itself, with a pediment to match. The style is neo-Grecian and such a very graceful introduction to this enchanting corner of the City. The east facing position offers, from midday onwards, oblique light, which casts shadows across the flat front of the building behind the portico. In this autumn scene I am capturing low, weak sunlight, which adds a delicacy of lighting, softening the dominant architecture and offsetting the verticals with gentle horizontal shadows.

In front of the building the statue of King Edward VII and fountains is a pale green complement to the warm stone building.

The Royal West of England Academy

The Royal West of England Academy, facing the Assembly Rooms, provides a contrast. This delicate architecture, renaissance in style, has slender columns, balustrades, statues and urns, yet somehow manages a unity of design and character. The ground floor frontage, added in 1913, is a rather too solid base, but nevertheless the building in total has an overall harmony.

Exhibitions, above and below stairs feature national and local artists and the night school classes held in the ground floor provide many a hardworking Bristolian with tuition, relaxation and another view of the world from the eyes of the artist.

The brief, classical, introduction to Clifton alters drastically as you leave the Victoria Rooms and enter Queens Road. I am always taken up short. The buildings you suddenly confront seem 'graceless'. They are examples from the 1930's, 40's, 50's with the Students' Union Building being a particularly monstrous example of how planning can throw sense and sensibility out of the window. Compared to its Georgian neighbours, this building marshalls the eye along featureless lines and angles on dead grey facings. The effect is dominating, intrusive and unwelcome.

The Students Union Building

Michael Edwards

Victoria Square

'Leafy Clifton' is epitomised by Victoria Square, which has here turned golden. The carpet of leaves matches the Georgian stone of the terrace just visible. This glowing afternoon has attracted an appreciative guest. Or perhaps he is waiting for some coins to be slipped into his cup.

The walkway cuts diagonally through the square and connects Clifton Village, via Boyces Avenue, to Queens Road. It is a favourite short-cut.

The Square itself is surrounded by the long renaissance-style terraces of Lansdown Place and the Royal Promenade, but they are hidden much of the year behind mature trees. The sheer scale of these nineteenth century palaces is consequently not often fully appreciated.

A quick sketch of a Clifton 'character'

Victoria Square, looking along the Royal Promenade buildings to the end of Lansdown Place.

Victoria Square, the archway connecting the walkway across the square to Clifton Village. The complex elevations of the building provide interesting problems of perspective.

Boyces Avenue, a busy parade of small shops and boutiques, including the well-known David Cross Gallery, specialising in marine paintings of the eighteenth and nineteenth century.

Tucked away in a small cul-de-sac off Boyces Avenue the Albion pub is a favourite haunt of university students. Each pub in Clifton seems to have its own particular clientele and the students have clearly adopted the Albion.

The Mall

The Mall is Clifton Village's heart. It is a true Georgian showpiece, not only the shops and buildings along its length, but also the long residential squares of West Mall and Caledonia Place extending from the Mall's centrepoint. Against the snow the earthy colours seem exaggerated. They add to the drama as does the steel grey sky. Stillness pervades. I felt like an intruder sitting in my car, sketching the quiet view.

In complete contrast, the painting of the dancers shows the village in its animated state. The annual Clifton Fair was an event planned by local activists and shop keepers originally to raise money to maintain the village's public gardens. People came in Victorian costume, games were set up, and activities of all sorts attracted a good turn out. Sadly, the fair is now history.

The famous Coronation Tap (shown left): Since I painted this picture, it has changed its colour but fortunately not its brew! Scrumpy cider is the speciality of the house. The pub faces squarely down the road, displaying some rather quaint graphic detail. The texture of the coloured plaster contrasts with the local stone of the houses along the street.

The Portland Vaults, a pub with some character, has now been rebuilt and converted into an off-licence.

Behind the tall Georgian terraces of Clifton are the corresponding town gardens containing a variety of trees and ornamental shrubs. Here in my garden at the back of the terrace, I take solitude and relative privacy for granted. Sometimes I can smell other people's barbecues or hear voices, but for the most part, the garden feels far removed from neighbours and traffic.

Michael Edwards

Worcester Terrace one frosty morning turned out to be a real bonus. The Catholic Cathedral appeared at the end of the terrace as an abstract, transluscent form rising out of a rosy shimmering mist. It might have been some U.F.O. firing its rockets ready to make an ascent.

Opinions vary about the Cathedral. The dual spire reminds me of a pair of rabbit ears on the alert. They can be seen poking up from many vantage points throughout Clifton. The listening church!

The Cathedral shares part of a landscape with Christ Church and you might say that they appear to be quite an odd couple! Christ Church, although built relatively late in 1885, is a classical example, yet I think it goes well with its modern friend. The fine steeple, apparently once intended as a tower, seems to have elements of Salisbury in its form and fits well into the composition of Christchurch Green, known as one of Bristol's loveliest. The green's gentle undulations are set off by a variety of sensitive architecture. Any potential clashes are mollified by the balance of these more dominant and pleasing elements: the church spire, the trees and fine terraces.

Christ Church

Clifton College

Mentioning the word Clifton in education circles immediately conjures up that famous institution Clifton College which has spawned so many scholars and people of note.

This view of the College across the green can be seen from College Road. The empty field is missing the cricket players. But old Cliftonions, whose memories are strongly etched with the sights and sounds of college life will no doubt imagine a game in play.

The varied skyline, with the green copper clad tower creates a somewhat jumbled effect, which is, however, rescued by the consistent use of the local red stone. The image it produces is appropriately Victorian: solidity, integrity and responsibility! The statues of Earl Haig and the knight in armour, both memorials to the Great War, help to compound the Victorian image.

How much, one wonders, does the architecture and design of buildings and the spaces within them create an ambience and style which moulds human personality, particularly in formative years?

Clifton Village remains a village, yet its diversity is its charm. In the Mall, there is haute couture and a bookmaker, the fishmonger and the jeweller, the antiques market and the newsagent and more. The village abounds with artists and musicians and students choose to live here too.

Clifton provides a cornucopia of life that fills the senses with pleasant memorabilia. People and architecture stick in the mind.

Clifton's cafes and pubs are well patronised, especially by the younger set. You can drop into Clifton at any time. Cafes are open, the coffee is on, snacks and meals are served in stylish or quaint surroundings.

Cafe interiors have held a fascination for artists from the time of the impressionists and before. No doubt it began as a move away from studio painting into a more natural social context. Silhouettes against streetside windows for instance, are interesting subjects. In this sketch, the students chatting away are quite oblivious to me drawing.

Inside the Dôme Cafe

Balconies, balconies, balconies of all shapes and sizes. They are everywhere. Some are dilapidated, but most are reasonably well painted and kept. Many are festooned with baskets of flowers and plants. The utility of such balconies, however, is limited. Virtually no one is ever seen on them, and being protected, as part of a listed building, they can be very expensive to maintain.

West Mall

Sion Hill

Caledonia Place

Canynge Square

West Mall In Winter

Brandon Hill

Moving away from the Village towards Hotwells and Bristol City Centre, the road drops sharply down Constitution Hill, producing a sudden view of an equally steep hill on the other side, Brandon Hill.

Started in 1897, Cabot Tower has a decorated pinnacle with balustrades, towers, statues and recesses in an ornate jumble on a Victorian square tower. It is a well known landmark and while not being of major architectural consequence, doubtless fulfills its purpose as a beacon admirably.

Michael Edwards

Royal York Crescent

Balconies sweeping into the distance in the UK's longest crescent building provide a challenge of perspective. Often compared to the Royal Crescent in Bath, Clifton's Crescent has a feeling of being lived in by real people – whereas in Bath one always expects bewigged waxwork models to be in every elegant drawing room or hallway.

Royal York Crescent sits on top of its mews, with the pavement 20 feet or more above the ground. The feeling of isolation on some grand piazza is immediately apparent with distant views over the harbour to Dundry Hill.

The skyline of the Crescent fluctuates wildly from the attempts over the years to increase the accommodation. Each house that was vast, is now divided into flats and apartments.

Fortunately conversion of the Regency interiors is currently handled with greater sympathy, but too late to save many of the corniches, the plasterwork, woodwork, fireplaces and doors which contributed to the original spacious interiors.

Just around the corner from Royal York Crescent is St Vincents Priory. This small building has unique windows with figures apparently taking the weight of the storey above.

The Zoo

The introduction to Bristol for motorists speeding along the M4 or M5 is a tourist sign with an elephant silhouette and the word Zoo. The only other attractions to rate such exposure are "Historic Harbour" and "SS Great Britain". Yet the Zoo is one of the smallest in acreage and totally surrounded by high stone walls. Apart from the screaming of baboons and occasional grunting from animals unknown, there is little evidence of the Zoo to the passing pedestrian in Clifton.

The Zoo is rightly famous both for its zoological excellence and attractive environment, it being a permanent flower show and park.

The Zoo is sited next to Clifton College, the ground it occupies is leased from the College. The college boys have special treatment with a low entry charge. Tales abound in local folklore of student pranks such as letting the baboons over the perimeter walls to terrorise the residents of Clifton.

The shallow pond with light filtering through the trees creates a stage for the flamingos – ballet style – to gracefully pirouette on tiptoe across the water.

For the artist a day at the Zoo with sketchbook and water colours is a rewarding experience. No long walks between animal pens and a backdrop of lawns, shady trees and excited children. The elephant's curiosity makes him lumber over to see if I have a bun in my pocket – though feeding the elephants is strictly forbidden.

Quick response with pen on paper is the name of the game when sketching the animals. Fortunately the penguins freeze when sunning themselves and the giraffe takes a lofty disinterest in everybody, artists included.

Clifton Suspension Bridge

This is Brunel's bridge – the symbol of Bristol itself. It straddles the famous Gorge at its most dramatic point, the craggiest, steepest and narrowest. To me the image is exciting as well as romantic . . . perhaps not dissimilar to an Andes footbridge. When the first stone was laid in 1836 and then even later in 1864 when it was completed, the motor car for instance was still to make a debut. The surprising fact is that Brunel's controversial bridge has stood the test of time, whereas its 20th century neighbour the Severn Bridge seems never to be without complaints and growing pains. The contrast must surely make a contented spirit of Brunel.

On the day I tackled this painting, a steel grey sky was boiling up. This was a perfect backdrop to heighten the romance and drama. Colours in the foreground stood out in unusual vibrancy, leaving the white tracery of the bridge strung delicately across the chasm.

In the wind that was blowing up, I was glad to be standing on terra firma opposite the Hotwells Terrace instead of on the Bridge, whose rocking motion would be sure to set off my vertigo alarm.

The Clifton Assembly Rooms